Salute to Sandy

Books by Dale Evans Rogers:

ANGEL UNAWARE

MY SPIRITUAL DIARY

TO MY SON

CHRISTMAS IS ALWAYS

NO TWO WAYS ABOUT IT!

DEAREST DEBBIE

TIME OUT, LADIES!

SALUTE TO SANDY

THE WOMAN AT THE WELL

———— ————

SALUTE
TO
SANDY

———— ☆ ————

Dale Evans Rogers

FLEMING H. REVELL COMPANY

OLD TAPPAN • NEW JERSEY

Scripture quotations included in this volume are from the
King James Version of the Bible.

By Way of Dedication

This is the saga of Sandy, who fought with the broken sword of the handicapped for his place in a world in which everything was for the strong . . . who tried so hard to be accepted by his fellows and to measure up to what he thought God wanted him to be . . . who tried so hard to get to Viet Nam where, he dreamed, he could at last prove himself in the service of God and country.

The splendid dream was broken by death before he could get there, and now Roy and I are flying toward the battle, in his place. He could not go; we go in his place, in tribute and salute to his trying.

This record of his trying and of our going I dedicate to him as one of the most courageous spirits I have ever known . . . and to the buddies to whom he threw the torch, as they fight the good fight in the jungles of Viet Nam.

Dale Evans Rogers

This Universally Beloved Pair

When John Daly presented Roy Rogers and Dale Evans on his *What's My Line* broadcast, he described them as "this universally beloved pair." That is correct.

The state of Texas wouldn't hold their friends; a million kids pray for them every night; more millions of parents call them blessed; they are greeted with cheers in the wards of children's hospitals; they are welcomed as joyously in Protestant churches, Jewish synagogues and Roman Catholic cathedrals. Their fan mail, up to now, totals better than fifteen million letters; close to two million people have bought Dale's books, and the royalties go to help underprivileged children. They rule an economic empire known as The Roy Rogers Enterprises; as King of the Cowboys and Queen of the West, they also "rule" a kingdom of kids to whom love means far more than the profit and loss of the Enterprises.

On their way to all this fame and fortune they broke all the rules laid down by the experts in the *How-to-Succeed* books. Neither went to college, where all would-be successes are supposed to go; they attended the School of Hard Knocks, and they say that God is President of that school; they thank the President often for what He taught them there. They insist that God, and not the salons of show business, has guided them to the top. Hollywood said God would never do it. Hollywood said that good guys never win.

For a long time it looked as though they wouldn't win. Roy was poverty's child; he never wore shoes, as he says, ". . . from early spring to late fall . . . 'til I was pretty grown-up." He dreamed of the day when he could eat as much as he wanted, and quit school at seventeen to help support a family desperately poor. To this day, he reads the *prices* first on the menus of swank restaurants. He loved stray dogs, abandoned cats, and injured animals, and brought them home ". . . just so they'd know that somebody cared." He cherished a great dream: some day, somehow, he'd be a doctor, 'cause doctors help people. He loved to sing and strum a guitar; he loved Hoot Gibson, the movie cowboy. Roy fought his way through grim years of denial and depression, picking peaches, cobbling shoes, shovelling gravel, singing for his supper with roaming, singing, musical combos, and hoping for the break that finally came when he signed a contract with Republic Studios in Hollywood, where he rode a horse and met Dale Evans.

Dale Evans could sing before she could read or write. At three she interrupted a church service to sing a solo; in her early teens she found herself married and deserted—left to support a baby boy. She struggled up through years of wracking loneliness and discouragement from little local radio stations to big-name bands, determined to make good as a professional singer, and determined that little Tommy would get his chance, if it cost her life. It nearly did just that, before she made it to California—and Republic Studios. When Roy met her there, he rubbed his chin in mixed doubt and admiration: he thought she was pretty, but "she sure didn't look like a filly who could ride a horse." He wasn't wrong; she hadn't been on a horse since she was seven years old. But she learned. It was good going for them at Republic, good and happy except for the tragic time when Roy's wife died, leaving him with two daughters and a baby boy. So when, fourteen months later, Dale and Roy were married, even Hollywood loved it.

But Hollywood still thought there was something wrong with some of their ideas about getting on in show business. Any sensible actor or actress, the movie folks said, should be glad to get any role, good or bad, inspiring or disgusting, that would help them up the ladder, and many a would-be star murdered his future in compromising his character. This Roy and Dale flatly refused to do. Never once did either one play a dirty part. They had that odd quality known as integrity. Offered a chance to read for a part in *Oklahoma!*, a surefire hit, Roy turned it down: "Who ever heard of cowboys dancing like that, or wearing cap pistols?" Told to play a drunken cowboy, he refused. "But we have a contract," stormed the producers. "You mean we *had* a contract," shouted Roy as he walked out. Years later, in Madison Square Garden, Roy and Dale decided to sing a religious song at the end of the show —"Peace in the Valley." The merchants who were selling Roy Rogers belts, chaps, and six-shooters to juvenile America went into a panic. One of them said, "You're making a mistake. You can't mix business and religion. If you do this, we won't sell your stuff." With one of the most profitable businesses in the country hanging in the balance, Roy said, "All right. Then *don't* sell it. Mamma (Dale) and I have talked it over, and we're going to sing it. Either that, or we'll just pack our trunks and head back for California." They sang it. The applause had the roar of thunder.

Back of that decision lay the fact that in God they had found peace, and they were determined to share that peace.

Said Dale to their manager: "You know, Art, if you live to get to the top, you often forget why you wanted to get there. Roy and I have prayed about this, and we asked God to show us the answer, and He did. If we get booed out of the arena for singing it, then that will be that. But we have decided that the only way we can really find ourselves is to lose ourselves in work for others. . . ."

They lost themselves more and more in their work for others as they grew in popularity, and in their belief that compassion was better than cash. Into their home came Robin, the little heroine of Dale's book, *Angel Unaware;* born retarded, born to die within two years, born to inspire mother and father into a new career of compassion for sick,

[10]

neglected, and underprivileged children from Texas to Korea. To this home came Dodie, Choctaw Indian-Scotch-Irish; Debbie, Korean-Puerto Rican, the pitiful orphan of the Korean war; Marion, picked up in an orphanage in Scotland, and at last, Sandy, the lovable waif who inspired this book.

So the Roy Rogers who longed to be a doctor and couldn't be that, finds himself healing hearts if not bodies, and the young mother who fought for a chance for Tommy opens doors of hope for suffering children and stricken parents, on a scale quite as colossal as anything Hollywood has ever known. She has held the Robins of other mothers in her arms; he has lifted blind and lame youngsters to sit in Trigger's saddle, as he talked them into courage. Roy's comment, when they adopted Sandy, is indicative of their minds and hearts: "Anybody can adopt a strong, healthy kid who has everything going for him, but *what happens to a little guy like that?*"

Death has taken three of their children: Robin, Debbie, and Sandy. They do not ask God "Why?" They accept suffering as *teaching*. In their world there are wars and rumors of wars, pain and agony, misery and trial, anguish, crucifixion and death; this they accept. They also accept the truth and fact that above the anguish, the battle, and the tragedy, they have a God of infinite mercy who helps them not to avoid it, but to walk through it to greater strength. In honor of Sandy they did not sit down to weep in despair; they flew to Viet Nam to talk

[11]

to the boys of the peace and power and compassion of God.

They are unique in our country and time; they have won a success and a popularity given to few, and won it through the practice of religious faith and principles which the "smart" ones in their business said was foolishness. What they have made, in this success, we do not know, nor care. What they have done, we can never forget.

The good guys never win? Says who?

FRANK S. MEAD
For the publishers.

Salute to Sandy

The Plane

We flew in a giant 707; aboard were 166 soldiers en route for the blood, sweat, toil and tears of battle. I could see the tops of their heads above the seats, and I knew that a lot of them would never come back. There was an occasional burst of laughter, but they were generally quiet with the resignation of the quietly expendable. Some talked; some sat still with that faraway look in their eyes; some slept like innocent children.

I was so tired, that first night out, that I could have screamed; I had been writing for six hours straight. My fingers were numb with writer's cramp and my brain just wouldn't work any more, so I leaned back and prayed for sleep. But next to me a uniform squirmed and wriggled, and the soldier in it wanted to talk. I couldn't see him very well in the semi-darkness of the plane, but my head snapped up when I heard him say something about Jesus Christ and Christianity being the only hope we had of getting through the mess in Viet Nam, and that he was glad that he could face whatever was ahead as a Christian soldier. He knew messes, well; he had been in Korea, and in Germany. I came wide awake at the sound of the voice. "He talks just like Sandy!" I looked closely— in his hair and eyes and jaw—in the spirit that spoke louder than his words—in that uniform, I *saw* Sandy. This could have been our boy.

In an aching silence, I looked at him and thought of the first time I saw Sandy, backstage in the Gardens in Cincinnati.

*   *   *   *

Roy and I with Wayne West and the Travelons at our departure from Los Angeles International Airport for Viet Nam, October 13, 1966.

Roy and Sandy with the foster parents, welfare official, and I in Judge Stubb's office, Covington, Kentucky, in October, 1952.

* * * *Sandy*

Sandy really got his little foot in the Rogers' door, unconsciously, just before our little Robin was born. That was in August of 1950. We were busy one day making plans for Robin when Roy said, "Look, Mama. If this baby is a girl, we've just got to adopt a boy to grow up with Dusty; poor Dusty's so surrounded with females now that he hasn't got a chance." Half listening, I agreed. (Any mother a week from childbirth will agree to almost anything!) Little did I know then that with the birth of Robin we would have the crushing burden of a mentally and physically defective child.

When she was a year old, Roy reminded me again of my "promise" to adopt a brother for Dusty (now three years old). My son

Tom was gone; Cheryl (Roy's first adopted child) was nine, and Linda Lou, his own natural child, was seven. I objected now, feebly; we couldn't think of adopting another, what with all I had to do in taking care of the ones we had, besides working in radio and TV, and public appearances. A mother can stand just so much, Mr. Rogers.

Robin died in 1952; a week or so later we were on our way to Madison Square Garden in New York. The show goes on, in this business, whatever your grief or problems. We stopped off in Dallas to visit my parents, and they took us out to Hope Cottage, the children's home from which Cheryl had been adopted, where we bumped into bouncing, black-eyed, black-haired little Mary (Dodie, to you), aged five months and ready for adoption. She was the exact opposite of Robin, who was pale, blonde, and blue eyed, and my arms ached for this child. Roy and I went into a huddle, and came out of it to suggest to the superintendent of the home that we should have her because she was of Indian, Scottish and Irish descent, and Roy was of Indian, Scottish, Irish, and German descent. What more could they ask? They said they would let us know; Mary was already "spoken for" by a Dallas woman of Indian blood. . . . Two weeks later we got word that "Mary" was ours; we could pick her up on our way home on October 28th, which was Dusty's birthday!

In New York Roy said, "Now, Mama, you promised a brother for Dusty. Remember?" (Like the elephants, he *never* forgets.) I mumbled an "O.K."; we'd start looking around for Dusty's brother. Before we could start that, we received a brochure from a home that was doing a wonderful work for European Jewish orphans, in bringing them into American homes. I called the home and asked about the handsome boy pictured on the cover of the brochure—and was told gently but firmly that these children must go into Jewish homes. Being Christians, we didn't qualify. It was hard for me to understand, and still is. I wondered what Jesus, with His Jewish background, would have thought about it. More sad than mad, I hung up the phone. (Often, looking at my adopted family, I have thought of how lives are changed by what seems merest accident. That little boy we didn't get—what became of him? We found Dodie by accident, too. When, where would we find a brother for Dusty? What a happenstance adoption is! Or . . . could it be God, directing it, sending some this way, some that way. . . ?)

We finished the New York engagement and started for home, doing a series of one-night stands on the way. In Cincinnati, we were resting one night before the evening performance at the Gardens. Roy was restless and preoccupied; he sat looking through a stack of letters, pulled out a telegram, and read it silently. He picked up the phone and I heard him say, "This is Roy Rogers speaking. I have just read your wire. . . . Of course I'd be glad to have you bring your little girl backstage to see us, tonight. You say you operate a home for handicapped children? . . . . Do you have a little boy about five years old who is eligible for adoption? . . . . Yes? . . . . Bring him along, will you?" Just like that.

During intermission they came: a woman pushing a wheelchair, holding a pitiful little girl with cerebral palsy, and, stumbling along beside them, a pale, wistful little boy—a small thin body topped by a rather large blonde head with enormous blue eyes. Roy went to him and held out his hand. Shyly, reaching out from a life of insecurity and fear, the boy took it, and, with a disarming grin and a surprisingly resonant voice, he said, "Howdy, pahtnah!" Something warm and wonderful flowed between boy and man in that handshake. Roy picked him up and put him on Trigger's back. To me it meant, instantly, that this boy was *in*—in our hearts, for good.

We got his history, in a one-minute resume: he had been born somewhere in Kentucky, and had been found, abandoned, in a motel where he had lived with his "parents" for eight months, in a state of serious malnutrition. Both mother and father were alcoholics, and so irresponsible and cruel that the courts had taken the child away from them. He had brothers and sisters; one was in an institution for the mentally retarded. This boy was only *physically* retarded. He had poor coordination, an obvious astigmatism in one eye, and an oversized and malformed head (thanks to rickets, which responsible parents would have corrected). He had never walked until he was two years old, and he had been in a spinal brace for many months. He had been badly treated and abused, and of course there might be some other physical handicaps develop, as a result of that, but the lady was quite certain that he was all right mentally. If we wanted him, it might be arranged.

We looked at him; he looked back with those great pleading eyes, a battered and beaten little refugee from drunken, brutal parents, pleading for a chance with a trembling grin of courage and hope, and we almost cried. We told the lady we would think about it, and pray about it, and let her know.

We wrestled with it, back in our hotel room. Was this the boy we wanted? How would he adjust to a new role as brother to Dusty—and how would Dusty react to him?

[24]

Suppose there were other defects, later? Would this be Robin all over again? And we kept seeing the brave grin on the little face, challenging the handicaps. Finally Roy said, "Mama, anybody can adopt a strong, healthy kid who has everything going for him. *But what happens to a little guy like this?* Let's take him."

We took him. We called the lady at the home—at 2 A.M. At 9 A.M. we were in a cab crossing the river between Cincinnati and Covington, Kentucky, and in less than an hour the papers were signed in the presence of a judge. Sandy watched us sign; then he leaped into Roy's arms with a big "Hi, Daddy!"

We hit the road for Dallas, to pick up his new sister Dodie.

Saigon

At 23:45 hours (fifteen minutes to midnight), we came in over Saigon's Tan Son Nhut Airport; I looked out of my window and I had the eerie feeling that we were cruising over the crater of hell. Down in that black murk below us were Americans—and a jungle crawling with a vicious enemy who would kill us if he could. There were little red flares down there, to the left on the rim of Saigon, to light up any "Charlies" (Viet Cong) with ideas of attacking. The plane dropped sharply; I gripped the arms of my seat, closed my eyes, and prayed.

We left the plane for a jeep that took us to the Meyer Kord Hotel, where the USO entertainers stay. We picked our way slowly through streets that frightened me even more than the sky had frightened me. They were unbelievably narrow streets, winding through a squalor that I had never seen before. There was a stench that was beyond description: too many people, too little sanitation. There were piles of refuse here and there in the streets, and some little children and grown-ups sleeping on the sidewalk, up against the old buildings. Now and then a guard loomed up in the darkness, signalling us to detour up or down another stinking, dusty, rutted street. Dear God, You never meant anybody to live like this!

As we started upstairs in the hotel, we heard a wild shout that stopped us cold; running toward us was a girl in fatigues, boots, and a green beret. It was Martha Raye— Lieutenant Colonel Martha Raye, if you please. If anybody ever deserved that rank, Martha does; if the boys out there had their say, she'd be a general. They worship her, and no wonder. The folks back home know her as a slaphappy, boisterous, zany comedienne; the boys know her as a gal who will go anywhere and do anything to help them—especially to help the sick and wounded. She

[28]

works around the clock in hospitals; she writes letters home for amputees; she sings at the drop of her jaunty, green beret, any hour of the day or night. Blind tired, she will go into her madcap act in the middle of the night for a gang just back from the fighting. What's more, she goes out where they are fighting, when she can get there. Only Martha Raye could do it. The boys call her "Colonel Mag," and don't say anything against her unless you want your head handed to you. She is on her fourth tour of duty in Viet Nam. I salute her: she is one of the greatest humanitarians I have ever known, a girl with a heart big enough to hold the whole Army, whose life has been anything but easy, giving her time, talent, and strength, and risking her life to make it easier for boys she never saw before and may never see again. She could have gone home long ago, but she begged the "brass" to let her stay until after Christmas.

Martha said, "Thank God you've come. You know, the boys, somehow, just couldn't believe you'd come all the way out here to entertain them. They need you and Roy—

they need what you have to say to them." She knew what was in our hearts to say to them; she knew about Sandy. She briefed us on what was ahead of us, told us what to expect, what to do. She was with us until 3:30 A.M.; she got less than two hours sleep and took off at six for the troops in the jungle. Many about to die would salute her.

In the morning we went out to see the town. We saw bicycles, all over the place. I swear there are more bicycles in Saigon than in all the rest of the world put together. Bikes, "cyclos" (rickshas driven by bicycles), motor scooters, cars—everything but pogo sticks. The river is jammed with small boats, sampans, and houseboats, packed in like sardines, with hundreds of jeeps and trucks rumbling along its banks, and that overwhelming, nauseating stench. There is more garbage than water, in that river.

Everywhere, young Vietnamese girls were riding behind boys on bicycles; with their soft olive skins and raven hair, I saw our little Korean Debbie in every one of them. In faces of the soldiers I saw Sandy. We saw soldiers sitting behind machine guns in front of military buildings, on tops of tanks, behind guns in the jeeps ahead of and in back of us, sent along just in case. . . . I worried. They laughed. Captain Jagielski, our official escort, must have known what we were thinking. He said quietly, "Morale is really high, out here; I think it's higher than it is among the folks back home." I thought so, too. I thought of the well-fed, clean, well-housed, safe, and comfortable civilians back home. I thought of the draft-card burners.

We did two shows that day, one at 2 P.M. and another at 6 P.M. One of them was in an old rice mill where they had to clean out three feet of rice chaff, dirt, and rubbish before our men could move in. The boys jammed both places. At the USO headquarters, they even stood on the stairs, in the hallways and on the street outside, and they clapped, and laughed, and sang. I sang with a lump in my throat. It was a bigger lump when Roy and I were given the honor of cutting the ribbon in front of a newly-built theatre. They called it "The Roy Rogers Theater." Yes, morale is high.

We had "noon chow" with the boys, and

what chow it was: fried chicken, broccoli, mashed potatoes, salad, pudding, lemonade, and that good old Army bread that has *body*. Don't worry about your boy's food in Viet Nam; it's the best. After chow, we took off for the Third Field Hospital—327 beds of pain, hope, and unconquerable spirit. Horrible burns, yellow-eyed malaria, men with hands, arms, and legs amputated, and smiles and confidence everywhere. If there's a hospital in the States like it, I haven't seen it. It was a completely humbling experience. There was one little six-year-old Vietnamese boy with fearful burns, one eye gone, both hands partially amputated—and a healthy grin. He bounced around the wards like a jumping-jack, from one American friend to another. A nurse said he had been playing with a hand grenade.

It hit me, full force, in that hospital, that we were fighting as much to give kids like this a second chance at life as we were to give our American kids a first chance.

* * * *

* * *   Sandy

We named him John David Rogers, but we called him "Sandy" in honor of his hair. Roy wasn't sure he liked the nickname, at first. He said, "Maybe later we can adopt another one and call him 'Filthy.'" He took the youngster to a boot manufacturer and bought him a pair of cowboy boots. Sandy was in seventh heaven; this made him like all the other boys, and he wanted to be like them. He wanted to sleep in those boots that first night, and we let him do just that.

His first meal with us in the hotel was something never to be forgotten; he ate as though food were going out of style—ate everything on his own plate and asked for what was left on ours. Roy said, "Take it easy, Sandy. There's more where that came from, so don't make yourself sick." Sick he was, most of the night. We had to call for an extra supply of towels.

In the morning we went over to Hope Cottage to pick up Dodie, and what a time we had there! Sandy wasn't quite sure he wanted to go into the Cottage; he knew what an orphan's home was, or could be, and he didn't want any part of it. He clung to me with a grip of iron, as though he were afraid we'd leave him there. While I was talking in the office with Mrs. Carson, the superintendent, he kept peeking in through the half-open door to make sure that I didn't run out on him. They would have liked to keep him there; he hypnotized everybody with his broad grin. We bundled up Dodie and ran for the plane to Los Angeles with our two "new ones." It was two months to the day since we had lost Robin. Who says the age of miracles is past? We had believed, then, that ". . . the Lord gave, and the Lord hath taken away . . ." (JOB 1:21), and our faith was justified. He had given us twofold for Robin.

When we landed at Los Angeles, I could

Roy and I with Sandy and Dodie, October, 1952.

Dodie, Debbie, Dusty, Sandy (age 11), and I on the ranch in Chatsworth, California.

see Dusty (now six) peeking out from behind the skirts of Ginny, his nurse. He knew we were bringing Dodie with us, and he wasn't sure he was going to like her; he knew nothing of Sandy. When he saw his new "brother," he was incredulous; I thought for a minute that he was going to take off and run out of there, but he didn't. He walked along with us, staring at Sandy as if he had come out of another world—which indeed he had. They talked in fits and starts on the way to the ranch, like a couple of little prizefighters sparring for position. Sandy tried hard to break the ice with a lot of chattering about his new boots, and he asked all sorts of questions about Dusty's toys when we reached home. Dusty reserved decision. He wasn't buying the "new guy" easily.

When it came time for bed, Sandy clung to me, afraid to be left there alone, in a strange place. I saw myself walking the floor with him all night, but gradually, as the room began to lose its strangeness, the grip on my neck relaxed, and with a kiss he slipped down into the bed, and fell asleep. Sandy was home. He slept in perfect peace, and my heart murmured, "You sweet Kentucky babe!"

Ginny went in to get the boys up in the morning and she found Dusty hiding his toys under the bed. When she asked him why, he said, "I just want to be sure they'll be here when I come home from school."

We decided not to send Sandy to school right away, but to keep him home until February; that would give him time to adjust to the new environment. It also gave us time to discover a lot about him that we hadn't expected. We bought him a tricycle, but he couldn't make his legs work together on the pedals. He couldn't stand on a chair without trembling; even that height frightened him. He had difficulty breathing; we found one nostril closed. Even the slightest discipline sent him into an emotional sweat. Emotionally aroused, he would vomit all night. There were other problems to cope with in the training of Sandy that were as much agony as ecstasy when they were conquered; looking back at it now, I treasure every minute of it as training for *me*, in Christian experience.

I am still hot with humiliation at some of the blunders I made, but grateful that God gave me the grace to say "I'm sorry, honey," when I was wrong.

We started rebuilding the poor little body by having the closed nostril opened so he could breathe normally. The surgeon said he had been injured when he was a baby, "either by a fall or a fist." Knowing what we did of his parents, we were sure it was a fist. A pediatrician, to whom we took him for a complete check, told us that the boy had many physical problems, but that loving care could do wonders with them, if we were patient enough.

A year later, worried about the continuing emotional sweats, we took him to Children's Hospital in Los Angeles for analysis and evaluation, and got more bad news. The electroencephalogram disclosed abnormality in the brainwave, indicating a slight brain damage. (The fist, again?) The doctor broke it to us gently: we must realize that Sandy would have "plateaus of learning," and that we must not expect continuous progress in his mental and emotional development. He was not mentally retarded, and he did not belong in an institution, but. . . .

We drove home with heavy hearts, with Sandy squirming between us, happily unaware of his doubtful future. Could we do it? Could we climb this high, hard hill? Could we do what had to be done? I realized that we could never do it alone, never—we needed the help of Another, and we both turned to Him for help. I whispered the Biblical promise I had learned long ago: "My grace is sufficient for thee: for my strength is made perfect in weakness" (II CORINTHIANS 12:9).

In February we enrolled both Sandy and Dusty in the second grade of a military school. To our surprise, Sandy loved it. He didn't exactly get straight "A's" in his lessons, but he worked like a little Trojan for what he got, and to keep up with Dusty. Even in his failures, he enjoyed it. He seemed to love being a little soldier.

We wondered; we brooded; we kept all these things in our hearts, where he couldn't see them.

The People
Out There

Martha Raye was right on two counts: when she told us that the going would be tough in Viet Nam, and that the boys were hungry for what we had to say to them. It was tough, first of all because of the smothering heat; more than one day we had to work with the thermometer standing at 108 degrees in the shade, and precious little shade; the humidity was 90 to 95. I'd say we have all lost ten pounds apiece. By "all," I mean the Travelon Combo from Apple Valley Inn that came along with us. I watched them one day, performing on an old flat-bed truck with a top made of old parachutes which the soldiers had rigged up for the show. There was Wayne West, who sings Western ballads to his own guitar accompaniment; we call him "The Wagon Master" at the Inn; the boys out here called him "just great." Jim Carney played bass guitar and did a rock 'n' roll that really got them. Charlie Lawyer plays the electric piano; we changed his name to "Chuck," for over here "Charlie" means the Viet Cong. Ti Gobert is an ex-Air Force drummer, and he really makes those drums talk. Dick Slye, who is Roy's cousin, plays electric guitar and yodels like a Swiss mountaineer. With "Paw and Maw" Rogers, there were seven of us. We didn't ask these Travelons to come with us; they volunteered. They splashed and floundered around in the mud and the rain, giving their best in two shows a day and sometimes more, and they never made a kick about anything. They would sing for two thousand in a big hall, or for a dozen in a mud hut. They never lacked an audience.

The audiences were enough, at times, to break your heart. We would look out over a sea of faces that were silent but not sullen, tired but somehow triumphant. We knew that we had to give them a good show, and something beyond a good show: something for the yearning deep within them. There were many Air Force men in these audiences: men just back from flights over enemies so cleverly hidden that they couldn't see them, men liable to capture or death from jungle-hidden guns. More than once we flew over territory pockmarked by bomb craters, and we knew that "Charlie" was down there waiting for a shot. These were flyers who faced that *every day*.

An airman gave me a card on which was printed a "Code of Conduct." It reads:

I am an American fighting man. I serve in the forces which guard my country and our way of life. I am prepared to give my life in their defense. I will never surrender my men while they have the means to resist. If I am captured I will continue to resist by all means available. I will make every effort to escape and aid others to escape. I will accept neither parole nor special favors from the enemy. If I become a prisoner of war, I will keep faith with my fellow prisoners. I will give no information or take part in any action which might be harmful to my comrades. . . . When questioned . . . I will make no oral or written statements disloyal to my country and its allies or harmful to their cause. I will never forget that I am an American fighting man, responsible for my actions and dedicated to the principles which have made my country free. *I will trust in my God and in the United States of America.*

That last line in the Code made me think again of Sandy; he talked like that, in almost the same words. He had this same attitude, this devotion, this courage. Of course, there were some people out there—and back home, too—who, right now, seem to be placing no trust at all in either God or country, but they are few. Yes, there were black-marketeers out there, making money out of the misery, just as there are profiteers back home, but don't let anyone try to tell me that the men doing the fighting are motivated by anything but the highest and noblest ideals. They were taught as children that the most precious possession in their America was *freedom*, and in Viet Nam they fight for that and for nothing else—for a free America and a free Viet Nam in a free world. They stand ready to die that this freedom "shall not perish from the earth."

There is often a religious drive behind this conviction. I saw it clearly the day we left Saigon to fly to Da Nang, when the plane suddenly "turned on its heel" and ran back to the airport we had just left. The hydraulic fluid was leaking, which meant that if we lost enough of it we would have no brakes, and we might not be able to get the landing gear down where it belonged. Roy and I were sitting up behind the cockpit, and from there we could see that we were flying dangerously close to the ground—directly over "Charlie!" The pilot didn't seem flustered, and as we sat in the lounge back at the airport, waiting for the plane to be repaired, I saw one reason why he wasn't flustered. On the wall of the lounge were written two "Flyer's Prayers." The one for the Jewish flyers read:

Almighty God, guide those who fly in thy heavenly abode and constantly risk their lives *to protect freedom for all mankind.* Lead them swiftly and safely to their destination and return them unharmed so that they may better serve Thee. May an end come soon to the present conflict and an era be ushered in that will make the prophetic words ring true: "Nation shall not lift up sword against nation; neither shall they learn war any more. Amen.

And the Christian prayer ran thus:

Almighty God, Who art the strength of them that put their trust in You, we pray You to guide and protect us as we fly on our assigned missions. Arm us with Your might and bless our efforts *to defeat the enemy of freedom, to bring a rapid end to this conflict and to win peace for mankind.* For the privilege of serving You and our beloved land, we thank You, and we praise You in the name of Jesus Christ our Lord. Amen.

The italics in these prayers are mine; I emphasize these words because I believe them emphasized in the hearts of the men who flew our planes, who manned the machine guns in our planes to protect us, who carried in our planes supplies for their comrades down there on the ground. "To protect freedom for all mankind . . . to bring peace. . . ." We went out there to help a little in boosting the morale of these boys and in strengthening their faith, only to find them strengthening *our* morale and faith. I commend these words to those middle-aged and complacent arm-chair generals and pacifists, who sit so safely back home complaining about their taxes, while these boys give their blood and their lives to defend something worth paying taxes *for*.

The same words might help some of those

"patriots" who would like to drive the chaplains out of the armed forces, in the name of freedom of religion. I suppose they are the same people who oppose prayer in the public schools, chaplains in Congress, and "In God We Trust" on our coins. They give me a grade "A" pain. Every time I met a chaplain out there, I thanked the free practice of religion which put him there. Just try suggesting to GI Joe that his chaplains be sent home, if you want double trouble. Why the troops should be denied the strengthening and consoling powers of religious faith in the shadow of death, I can't figure out. It is nonsense—and blasphemous.

On the beach at Chu Lai, we found a beautiful native-type chapel built by the Marines in the area, under the guidance of their chaplain—a dedicated man, if there ever was one. He had once been a singer with the Fred Waring ensemble, at home. We sat in a pew facing the altar; through an open window we could see the rolling ocean, and we thought of the mercy of God being like "the wideness of the sea." Hanging over the chancel on a long wire was a stained-glass cross bearing the form of the One crucified 2000 years ago. There was a terrible truth in that figure: it was topped by a crown of barbed wire! One of the Marines had made it out of glass from an old, ruined church; he had pasted the glass on plastic and enclosed the whole thing with wire. The chaplain stood beneath that cross to conduct his service. I can never forget it. Besides conducting religious services and ministering to the men, the chaplain was in charge of their entertainment. He worked hours that would kill an ordinary man. I was out there on one fast trip; this man was there in the name of God, twenty-four hours a day. I salute the chaplains. God sent them there, and no man has any right whatever to take them out of there.

We sat in another service at Qui Nhon, in a chapel called "The Chapel of Peace." Peace! There was a little electric organ played by a Vietnamese soldier who was substituting for the regular organist. He was really an accordionist, and this was the first time he had ever tried to play an organ. He did very well until he came to the Doxology, which he didn't know. I wanted to jump up and offer to play it for him, but hesitated out of fear that I would offend him. This little fortress of the faith stands in sharp contrast to the surroundings of depressing poverty, mud, and misery, and throws the gauntlet of faith's serenity into the face of Mars. It is mute peace in the midst of tribulation. The chaplain preached a sermon that really "rang the bell" in my heart. He challenged his congregation to remember the Good Samaritan on the battlefield! He questioned the piety that refuses to stoop and lift. He built an altar in the heart of every listener. Who would rob the boys of *that?*

General "Monk" Meyer had a hand in building this chapel. He is quite a man, and he goes all out in the religious department—the perfect example of reliance upon religious faith which runs from top "brass" to rookie private. In Da Nang, we had lunch with General Walt, who is senior commander of the Marines in Viet Nam. Da Nang is only about seventy-five miles south of the Demilitarized Zone, and there is action in all directions, danger every second. Yet when we sat down to this delicious lunch, the General offered prayer—not just "grace," but *prayer*. Behind him, as he ate, was a large painting of the Last Supper. For the second time in my life I asked for an autograph—his. I brought home his name and witness on the flyleaf of a New Testament presented to me by Lambda Theta Chi, the Christian married women's society (standing for "life through Christ"). To this General, Christ *is* life.

The most terribly present of all the people out there is "Charlie"—the enemy, the Viet Cong. You never take your mind off "Charlie"; if you do, you're dead. He is as sly, sneaky, and deadly an enemy as we have ever faced. Thanks to his Oriental physique and characteristics, he infiltrates without any trouble at all; you just can't tell him from a loyal Vietnamese. I remember landing at Da Nang in a teeming rain; it fell in sheets and blankets, and everything got soaked. When we went out to do our five-o'clock show, we found our guitar amplifiers soaking wet, and that meant that the player would be electrocuted the second he touched a string. A marine brought a hot-air blower and we waited thirty minutes while our audience—men who had been on the alert from midnight to daylight—stood or sat in the rain. They were dog tired, but they knew that "Charlie" was just over the hill, maybe even in their midst, and they couldn't relax for a minute. It's always like that.

"Charlie" is often innocently hired by our forces as a laborer, or one of their women or girls is hired as cleaning woman or waitress. Captain Ayres told us about an old woman who was drawing water out of a well, when a group of Marines came along; she whirled suddenly, with a gun in her hand, and started firing. Lucky for the Marines that she was a rotten shot; she hit nobody, and they left her dead by the well. Then there was the disguised "Charlie" hired as a laborer who got up in the middle of the night, did his dirty work, and sneaked back to his cot before he could be identified. (They caught him, later.) Sneaky little men, the Viet Cong: they

[52]

reminded me of the gophers we see on the prairies, slithering around in their underground tunnels. At Camp Holloway, they slipped through our guards in the night, and planted satchel-charged dynamite bombs in the helicopters along the airstrip; when the pilots, next morning, started their engines, they were all blown to bits in less than thirty seconds. There is no neatly marked-out front line; "Charlie" is everywhere.

I can still close my eyes and see the native Vietnamese—the people who *live* there: the poor, hungry, frightened, sick, shelterless victims of a war that has been going on for longer than they can remember. There has been war in this country, steady war, for twenty years; many a child and youth has never known a day without battle. It was a sickening sight . . . the helpless, crying children . . . the little girl with club feet (straightened out in a U.S. hospital!) . . . another little girl with both arms blown off . . . the old man trudging along to market with a skinny rooster under his arm . . . old men and women with the "black smile" caused by chewing betel nuts,

[53]

which contain a mild narcotic that deadens the pain of rotting teeth . . . children bare from the waist down, wallowing in the mud . . . the old blind woman standing in the doorway with a naked baby (grandson?) in her arms . . . the eight-year old girl walking half a dozen smaller children down the street, holding them in check with a long rope thrown around them like a lasso . . . the teen-age girls sitting in doorways reading Asian comic books, girlie books, love-story books, movie magazines. We look at these people, and they look back. The young people smiled (sometimes) openly, hopefully, but many of the older ones gave us cold, hard, inscrutable stares of suspicion and distrust. Can you blame them? They have had years of being deceived, exploited, tortured, and slaughtered. Why should they trust anybody?

Several of our officers told us that they are beginning to trust us. Maybe it's because they see their children healed in American hospitals; they have seen hospitals built for *them*, where there was only death before. They have seen orphanages built for children who, in earlier days, died alone on the streets. They have seen recreation centers erected for kids who never knew how to play, and American agricultural specialists helping Vietnamese farmers coax more out of their soil. This is a part of this war; it isn't just another war of attrition and destruction; it is the building of a new free Viet Nam.

Sandy would have loved it. I think he would have loved building schools and orphanages as much as he would have loved driving a tank. I talked to the boys about Sandy, of why he wanted to get to Viet Nam, of how grateful we are that, though he made a mistake and paid for it with his life, he believed with all his heart in the teachings and way of Christ, and in America and her way of life. I told them simply and plainly that I, too, believed this, and that I had dedicated my life to it, even as he had.

Not so long ago, there was a big rock and roll hit record called, "I Can't Get No Satisfaction," and there was more truth than poetry in that for the teen-agers. They seek security and fulfillment in their lives, but they will never find it, never satisfy their thirst for truth and purpose in their lives until they touch the Source of it all in the person of the Christ who said "Whosoever drinketh of the water that I shall give him shall never thirst . . ." (JOHN 4:14). I believe it because I have experienced it. I told them that, often within sound of battle. One night at Da Nang three flares lit up the sky; "Charlie" was at it less than four miles from where we stood. Probably often, I didn't get through to them, but a lot of times I did. I know. They told me so.

The best news I heard out there was that God was not dead out there. They are betting their lives on that.

✳   ✳   ✳   ✳

Sandy at the age of twelve.

The Rogers family waiting to go on stage at the Ohio State Fair in August, 1956.

Sandy and Dusty with Roy near the farm of Roy's childhood at Duck Run, Ohio.

Roy, Sandy, and I with Recruiting Officer at Fort MacArthur, San Pedro, California, in February, 1965 (U.S. Army Photograph).

* * * *Sandy*

Sandy and Dodie were dedicated to Christ in the St. Nicholas Episcopal Church in Encinco, California. Sandy was deeply responsive to the occasion, and he moved easily and naturally in the activities of the church. He said sweet, sincere little prayers, talking as frankly and naturally to God as he did to the family. In the several churches we attended, as we moved from place to place, he was active with Dusty and the girls in youth activities, and with them, when Billy Graham came to Los Angeles, he rededicated himself to Christ. Many were the times I saw him kneel at the church altar, and I was proud. He didn't have to be forced, in all this; he did it eagerly, because he wanted to do it.

This was his religious development; there

was another development which had nothing to do with the church. He and Dusty were so full of vim and mischief that I sometimes swore that they had been sent to make life miserable for me. If there was any trouble around anywhere, this pair was in it. They went shopping with me, riding in the big back seat of the car, but they didn't help me shop. They would wrestle around in the seat, yelling at each other like a pair of Apache Indians. I tried to play the part of referee in those bouts, but they never paid much attention to the referee until I put a good sized switch in the front seat, and used it in the back seat whenever the situation called for it. I used it even in downtown Los Angeles traffic! One day the switch really connected with a bare little leg and Sandy announced, as spokesman for both athletes, "Mawm, we're going to leave home."

I wasn't frightened at the prospect. I put down the switch and said quietly, "All right, boys. When we get home, I'll help you pack." Dead silence in the wrestling pit. Then Dusty said, "Well, maybe we'll wait a year."

"Don't let me detain you, gentlemen." No reply.

We were just about to leave the house one morning to go out on location at the Iverson Ranch (where many western films are made). I had just put on my heavy western belt when Ginny called to me: "Dale, you'll never believe what those boys are up to. Take a look out of the window." I had been told previously that they had been opening the mailboxes along the street and filling them with assorted rocks, dirt, and trash, and I should have done something about that, but for some reason I didn't. Millie, my hairdresser, and I went outside and looked up Amestoy Avenue, and to my amazement beheld our two cherubs having a field day pulling out letters and examining them, leafing through magazines, and using the mailboxes as targets for their handfuls of rocks. I snapped off my belt and took off after them a la Simon Legree. I should have known better. They ran like a couple of track stars, yelling like banshees as I swung and missed, swung and missed. When I came to my senses and realized that I was putting on a ridiculous performance, I went slowly back to the house, where Ginny and Millie were holding their sides in laughter. I never tried that again; neither did the boys. Come Sunday morning, they sat with me in church, a pair of sinless little saints sprouting wings. I reckon it happens in lots of families. It's part of growing up.

Roy had his moments with them, too. One afternoon I heard a wild roar from the shed where he kept his beautiful racing boat. Someone had pulled every inch of the rubber from the dashboard of the boat, and if someone had taken a shot at him from ambush, father Roy could not have been as mad as he was in that shed. Court was held in the living room—for three days running. His Honor cross-examined, pleaded, cajoled, and threatened them with everything up to and including the electric chair, but he might as well have been talking to the stone faces on Mount Rushmore. It was definitely a one-way conversation. By the third day, he'd had it. He said, "OK, boys. I know one of you did it.

Roy entertaining for a capacity audience at the Saigon USO in October, 1966 (Dale Evans-Roy Rogers Show; USO-Hollywood Overseas Committee Tour).

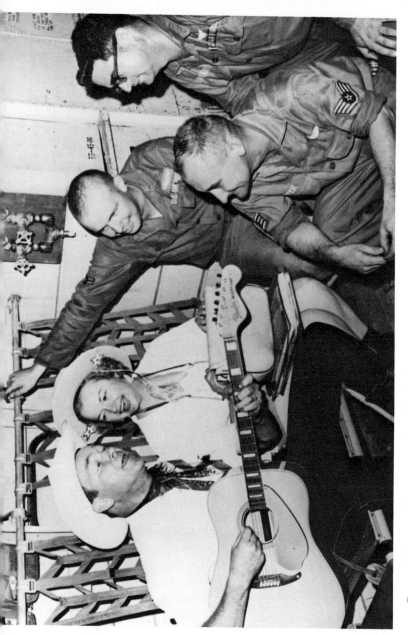

Roy and I entertain crew members A.2.C. Crawley, S.Sgt. Sutek, and T.Sgt. Miller of an Air Force C-123 Provider (Dale Evans-Roy Rogers Show; USO-Hollywood Overseas Committee Tour)

If you don't want to 'fess up, I'll just have to give both of you a good licking." He fingered his belt. Sandy piped up, "I did it, Dad." He was like that. He always came through, in the pinches.

All of which means that in the live-and-have-fun department, Sandy was a perfectly normal boy. He loved life, even when it was packed with trouble. Considering his pre-Rogers background, he was doing pretty well, with that attitude.

They were still quite young when we enrolled them in a military school in Pasadena, and then in the Ridgewood Military Academy in Woodland Hills, near Chatsworth. It was during the days in these schools that Sandy began to show an almost fanatical interest in anything military, anything connected with Kentucky (his native state), and the Civil War. He called himself "The Rebel," and defended the confederacy as the Greeks defended Thermopylae. On his thirteenth birthday, I remember, all he asked for was a confederate uniform! He would click his heels and yell at Dusty, "The South shall rise again!"

and they argued endlessly over the merits of Lee versus Grant.

It was funny. It was also a pattern. Even as a tot, he loved to play with toy soldiers, guns, tanks, and airplanes; especially tanks. He would sit for hours on the floor maneuvering his armies and tank corps, fighting great battles, and always winning great victories. Now, in school, he was pretty sad in math and English, and good in history. He wasn't as quick as Dusty to grasp things in the classroom, and it took him a lot longer to make the rank of Private First Class—but he made it. He took his many failures in stride, got up and went at it again. Every birthday and Christmas, he asked for books on military history; the names of generals, battles, weapons, and wars rolled off his tongue glibly, and he knew what he was talking about. With his allowance he bought countless little tanks, and tank kits to assemble, and little rubber drivers and gunners to go with them. He looked up at me one day and said, very, very seriously, "Mawm, some day I'll learn to drive a *real* tank." There was a prophecy in the words that I did not understand then; I understood it later.

Tanks, soldiers, and food—I'm not sure which he loved most. I can still hear the kitchen door burst open at four-thirty in the afternoon and hear him shout, "Mawm! What's for dinner?" He would bounce over to the stove, lift the lid on every pot and sample its contents. He hated liver; he could smell it cooking a mile away, and he shunned it like the black plague. Mashed potatoes, yes; the pile on his plate looked like Mount Whitney. After every meal, we could always expect Sandy to stand up at his place and say, "That was a good meal, Granny (Mrs. Miner, our helper). Thank you." Not many youngsters do that. His background was bad, but the instincts of the gentleman were in Sandy.

Occasionally we took the boys along to perform with us in our rodeos and state-fair shows. One day Roy decided to drive to the Milwaukee State Fair with them in the car; he thought they should see this great land of ours, this beautiful America. It was one of those good ideas that just doesn't work. Roy

[69]

was disgusted when they slept most of the way there. He'd wake them up to see something he thought they shouldn't miss, but America the beautiful was a total loss, so far as they were concerned. They had a pair of big white rats which only they could love; I had something less than love for them when they chewed up the bottoms of the expensive draperies in their room. On the trips, they kept them in a bird cage, but experience taught them that keeping them in a shoe box made it easier to get by the desk in motels and hotels. On the way home after one show, in the plane, there was quite a commotion in the shoe box stowed away under the seat. When the lid came off we found that mother and daddy rat had presented us with a passel of babies. Pandemonium reigned. It was almost as bad as the night they discovered a bat in their room in one of the older hotels. You could have heard the racket in Peking as they went after him and finally cornered him in the bathtub. There was hardly enough left of that bat to wash down the drain.

It was fun watching them grow up. And

there was worry. We noticed more and more that Sandy was having difficulty keeping up with Dusty and his playmates. He and Dusty loved to wrestle; Sandy always lost. He couldn't keep up in their footraces. He went out for Little League, and he never made a team, but he carried bats and water pails and loved it. At touch football he didn't seem to know how or where to run, or how to dodge quickly, but he kept on playing. We sent him to remedial-reading school for awhile, but it didn't do much for him. Roy tried to teach him to drive the jeep; he just couldn't get the right foot down on the right pedal at the right time. Roy took Sandy and Dusty out on a trap-shooting range, to teach them to shoot: something western boys learn to do. Dusty was a good shot from the start, but Sandy couldn't master that shotgun, to save his life. At last, rather than embarrass him, Roy stopped taking them out. We bought him barbells, for exercise and to help develop coordination; they didn't help, either.

In moments of failure he would clown—go into a comedy act. In one of our shows we gave him one short line to speak; he got it all twisted up before he was half way through it—all of a sudden he pulled his hat down almost to his chin and yelled, "Mawm! I goofed!" The crowd roared; they thought it was funny and clever, but Roy and I knew it was a cover-up to hide his embarrassment.

He did some things that shocked us, completely unconscious that he had said or done anything out of line. There was, for instance, that embarassing moment in the Chapel in the Canyon. The boys at the Chapel used to get together for a little touch-football Sunday afternoons; at six o'clock they came to the Chapel for a pot-luck supper and an evening service. Dodie and I got there late; we saw Sandy on the other side of the sanctuary, sitting with his friends. When the pastor invited those who wanted to pray to come to the altar rail, Sandy and the others went down the aisle. He knelt—and to my horror I saw that he was barefoot. He'd left his shoes in the park. "Just as I am, I come, I come!" That's what they sang, and that's how he went—just as he was. Even when I scolded him for it, he couldn't see anything wrong with it, and as I look back at it now I think he was probably right about it. I think the good Lord doesn't want us to wait until we're all shined up and decked out in our best clothes before we come to Him. I think God understood Sandy that day better than I did.

At sixteen he and Dusty got a job digging ditches for a real-estate promoter; Sandy spent every cent of his earnings for an old Civil War sword at the Army Surplus Store in Canoga Park. He polished it every day, sometimes five times a day.

At sixteen he was in love—unrequited love, alas. He could see the girl but the girl couldn't see him. He was crushed, and he had nothing to live for. He wouldn't be comforted; this was the *end*. I tried to explain that God had just the right girl waiting for him, somewhere, and that he must learn to wait. He didn't believe, it, but time took care of it, and he met "Miss Right"—Sharyn, whom he first respected, then adored and loved. They were inseparable. He left her, unhappily, to spend a nine-day vacation with Mawm, Dusty, Dodie and Debbie in Hawaii —where he spent every evening on the beach in front of the Moana Hotel, talking with the servicemen stationed in the area. He said he enjoyed being with these men in uniform and he talked a lot about how he'd like to serve his country in that uniform. I thought it was just talk. It wasn't.

A month later our beloved little Debbie was killed in a bus accident. Roy was in the hospital in a serious condition, following a spinal operation, and I was left to face it with the other children. The children were marvelous. Both Sandy and Dusty felt my pain; it got into their hearts, and there was a silent, sacred, spiritual, comforting bond between us without which I think I would have collapsed. Shortly thereafter, Roy leased the Apple Valley Inn near Victorville, California, and we moved out there.

One night before we moved to Apple Valley, Sandy sat down with Roy and me, and I knew from the look on his face that something important was about to happen. He had something on his mind. He said, "Look, I'm not making good grades in high school, and . . . well, I'd like to enlist in the Army. I want that more than anything else in the world." (I thought in a flash of the toy soldiers on the floor, the little tanks, the military books on the shelf.) "I'll be eighteen in June, and I could wait till then, but I'd like to go now. But I don't want to go unless you want me to —not without your blessing. I have one more year in high school, but I promise, if you'll let me, to get my diploma in the service. I want an army career."

In the silence that followed he blurted out the truth lying at the bottom of it all: "I want to *prove* myself in the army." That was it.

What could we say? What do mothers and fathers say, in such moments? What *can* they say? We said, "Go, and God go with you." And Sandy said, "I'll make you proud of me."

The next morning we watched him go. Granny Miner drove him out through the ranch gate, and he waved until they were out of sight. To this day Granny feels bad about driving him to the recruiting station, as though, somehow, she were responsible for what happened later. Of course she wasn't; he could not yet drive a car himself, and she was only helping him to fulfill the dream of his young life.

Frankly, we doubted that he could ever pass the physical examination, but he did. We doubted that the army would take him when they had the facts about his background, and his handicaps, but he told them nothing about all that, and he got by. We signed the release for him and saw him off for basic training at Fort Polk, and my heart was as heavy as lead.

I said to Granny, "Sandy will never be home again."

Notes From My
Viet Nam Diary

I saw and heard and felt so much in Viet Nam that I couldn't possibly write down *all* of it. But I did keep a diary of each day's happenings, and maybe I can give you some of the highlights of the trip by just quoting from the diary. It was all written in planes, or waiting in airports, or backstage at our shows, or at midnight in "quarters," so it is something of a hodgepodge, but here goes. . . .

Landed this A.M. at An Khe, where we found the First Cavalry. We came in so low that I vow we scraped the tops of the trees. The pilot had to reverse his props the second we touched ground, and my stomach made contact with my spine. Navigator told us later that we just barely cleared a mountain ridge from which "Charlie" loved to take pot-shots at our planes. Roy says he is going to examine the belly of the plane; he thinks we may have lost it somewhere in those trees.

Just shook hands with a company of men leaving for the jungle. They'll miss our show, so that was the least we could do. Saw no fear on their faces: only grim resolve. Here and there a young lip trembled a little, probably from nostalgia at the sight of "home folks." I was so choked up I could hardly talk. I was relieved a little when Wayne West let out a wild, delighted whoop, on the airstrip. His foster son (Wayne didn't know he was here) was waiting for him! The boy will travel with us for a few days, thanks to a commanding officer with a heart.

Met a boy we had known in the church at Burbank. He thanked me for my witness for Christ, and the words about Sandy. He said, "I think I'm a Christian. I do a lot of things I know I shouldn't do, but I'm trying. It isn't easy, out here. . . ." Of course it isn't. I find it hard to condemn any of them. I told him that his emotions were no guide to the salvation of his soul. Isn't it too bad that so many people put all their trust in their emotional reactions in religion, instead of trusting in the promise of Christ that ". . . him that cometh to me I will in no wise cast out" (JOHN 6:37)? There is great mercy and forgiveness, as well as judgment, in Christ. This boy will be all right. He's reading his Bible.

I get as much kick out of hospital visits as I do in putting on our shows. Just met an eleven-year-old girl in hospital with a huge hole in the left side of her face. I could see her tongue through the hole. She had been hit by shrapnel three years ago; one of our men found her in a jungle village and brought her in for plastic surgery. The people, the natives, get the same hospital care that our soldiers get. In the same hospital, a young soldier grasped my hand and said, huskily, "Ma'am, I was in Sandy's company in Germany." "Were you with him—that night?" "No, but I wish I had been. It

wouldn't have happened if I'd been there."
"He tried to be a good soldier, didn't he?"
"Ma'am, he *was* a good soldier." He was the
third boy to say that.

Just had after-show refreshments in a tent.
A soldier came running in to report that nine
"Charlies" were sitting on a hillside about
200 yards from us all during the show. A pla-
toon went out and got them. Three of them
were armed to the teeth. Wonder whether
they liked the show?

We are loaded down with presents from
everybody. One of Sandy's pals gave us a
lovely Vietnamese picture on which he had
written, "In memory of John." We have
carved and painted insignias from every outfit
we have entertained. Roy has a pile of weapons
for his gun collection: a machine gun, three
cross-bows, and enemy rifles. Hope we can
get them home.

Heard some good stories at An Khe. The
commander of a VC division was wounded
and captured, then treated by our doctors.
He was a surly one who expected torture, but
the treatment he got won him over so com-

pletely that he made a tape recording in which he pleaded with VC groups in the jungle villages to surrender. And a lot of them did. Another captive was beating our men at card games in the hospital. He defected with enthusiasm. Once a VC defects, we learned, it's for keeps.

"Charlie" is certainly tricky. He moves in small groups, through jungle bush and the little jungle villages. One of our helicopters was fired on by such a small group, fired back, and landed to pick up a young girl who was lying on the ground, too weak to get up and run. She had been enslaved by the VC for some weeks, and she was nearly dead. "Charlie" had forced her to carry his heavy equipment; she had deep gashes on both her shoulders. When our men ran towards her, she pointed to a little cluster of trees and screamed, "Kill! Kill!" In the trees were four "Charlies" waiting for a clear shot. The Americans fired first.

The longer I am here the more I realize *why* we are here, and why we should be doing what we are doing. Dedicated doctors are volunteering four months of service *to the civilian population*. Until you see these undernourished people in their poverty-stricken environment, you can't understand what such service means. Many babies die at birth; many are born with defects due to inadequate diet during pregnancy. Our military doctors treat them in off-duty hours, when they are not busy in the Army hospitals. It warms your heart.

We *are* our brother's keepers! Let none of us despise the American policy of caring for the sick and hungry of the world. Yes, it is unfortunate that so much of our dollar aid gets into wrong hands, but most of those dollars still feed the hungry and heal the sick. It is Christianity in action.

When you watch the younger American generation perform out here, you get the idea that this younger generation isn't as foolish and rebellious as we have been led to think. Their ranks have been infiltrated by the same sneaky communism that has infiltrated into Viet Nam. "Charlie" sneaks in and attacks when he thinks we are asleep, and the agents

Roy giving an autograph to SP5 Michael Schroeder at the USO in Saigon in October, 1966 (Dale Evans-Roy Rogers Show; USO-Hollywood Overseas Committee Tour).

An audience at the USO in Saigon which included patients from the Seventeenth Field Hospital (Dale Evans-Roy Rogers Show; USO-Hollywood Overseas Committee Tour).

of the international communist conspiracy have done the same sneaky thing at home, infiltrating into schools, youth groups, trade unions, politics—everywhere. I'm sure of it. There has been a subtle brainwashing going on, or being attempted, by the communists. When their hand is called, they run to hide behind the Fifth Amendment. They have done a lot of harm, and we parents are more to blame for letting them get away with it than the younger generation is to blame. But when the boys get out here, they show their real colors and really come through, working and fighting twelve, fourteen, even eighteen hours a day, defending their own country, and defending the Vietnamese from this insidious invasion. Now I know why Sandy wanted to come here, and why so many of them are volunteering to extend their tours of duty. An understandably bitter officer said to me this morning, "What we used to call patriotism is now called extremist action." If this is the case, I go along with Walter Brennan, who said, "If being a patriot means you're a right-winger, then I'm out on the end of the limb."

Move over, Walter. I'm with you. If the demonstrators at home are screaming about our being in Viet Nam, I suggest that they get in line with a worthier cause: that they come out here and demonstrate for the cause of human freedom with "Charlie" just over the hill, instead of stabbing our men in the back with their childish marches and riots at home.

No one wins a contest with a charging dog by turning and running away from that dog; the more he runs, the more the dog is encouraged to attack. Uncle Sam is fighting a global conspiracy, and you don't fight that with a placard in your hometown street. This enemy starts brushfires all over the country, hoping to drain the United States of money and manpower. One of them has said, "We will take America . . . she will fall like a ripe plum into our hands." *Will she?* It is for us to decide whether we remain free under God or enslaved under communism.

Take it or leave it, that's how I feel. It's a lesson taught me in Viet Nam.

I was asked to say something to the boys about the race problem. It has moved from the States to Viet Nam. I hesitated, but I knew I had to do it. Simply, I started with Paul's words to the Greeks. "[God] hath made of one blood all nations of men . . ." (ACTS 17:26), with the thought that in his sight the fact that a man is a Greek, a Jew, a Negro, or a white doesn't mean very much; that it isn't the nationality or the color of the skin that counts, but the quality of the character and the soul. I said that the greatness and strength of the United States was due, in part at least, to the strengths and abilities of people of all nationalities and cultures, of all racial and religious backgrounds; that historically we had welcomed peoples of all races, creeds, and colors, and that no real American held any prejudice, bitterness, or bigotry toward *any* of those people. The race riots at home were a disgrace, particularly at a time when we need the help of every man in the nation.

A fine looking Negro soldier shook hands with me afterwards, and thanked me; he said, "I'd like to do something about this race problem in the service, but I don't know just what to do, or how to do it." Between signing autographs, I said to him, "Son, the next time someone starts a racial 'ruckus' with you, or with someone else, just remember that he isn't very smart. Do you know Rafer Johnson?" (Rafer is one of our greatest American athletes; he's an Olympic champion, and he's a Negro.) His face beamed: "Rafe's my hero!" I told him then that I had heard that Rafer Johnson had this to say about the race problem, to huge audiences all over the United States: "Faith in God and the practice of the principles of Christ are the only answers to the race problem." Pattern your approach to the problem after Rafer, soldier! I do. He's a hero to me, too.

Actually, I'm not worried over the race problem among the men out here. When they eat in the same mess, sleep in the same barracks, face the same enemy in the same jungle, help each other when they're hurt . . . well, that washes out a lot of the "problem." Too bad it takes a war to do it!

Had a funny one last night. Roy was introducing me, and he said, "Now I want you to meet a little lady who means a lot to me. She is the mother of my children and a good trouper in show business. Come this next New Year's eve, we will have been married nineteen years." All of a sudden, a boy in the audience yelled out, "Hey, Roy! Would you like to re-enlist?" It almost broke up the show. I laughed so hard I couldn't sing.

A half-intoxicated boy came up to me later and said, "Miss Evans, I saw your show and enjoyed some of it, until you started 'talking gloomy' about your boy drinking in Germany. You're talking nonsense, and I don't go for it; I walked out." I tried to quiet him down but he wasn't being quieted. He exploded with this: "Why don't all these women (mostly old maids) lay off us about our drinking in the service? What do they know about it? Do they know what we have to do? Do you know what it's like to kill a man? Our Cobra outfit is responsible for killing 400 'Charlies.' How do you think we feel when we come back from a picnic like that? About all we have waiting for us, to help us forget it, is a bottle. That's the only way we have to let off steam. Would you and your women deprive us of that?"

It was a good question—one we had better think about, and hard. I could only tell him that I could understand his revulsion to the job he had to do, and that I appreciated his frustration, *but that liquor was no solution to any of it.* Was it any better when the hangover wore off? He stared at me, smiled, and turned to a buddy standing nearby and shouted, "Give her your Cobra pin." When the buddy hesitated, he roared, "I said give it to her." The buddy did. I think it is the most appreciated decoration I ever received.

It's hard for a Christian to justify this business of killing. I feel inadequate in trying to deal with it. There are times when I just want to stand and yell, "No, no, *no!*" Then I remember that Christ said we were to preach the gospel to every nation, that there will always be wars and rumors of wars, and I know that if these enemies of ours succeed in winning, millions will never hear of that gospel. Only a sadistic mind *enjoys* killing. I do not believe that we as a nation have ever gone into any country to kill people for the fun of it, nor to make them act or believe as we act and believe, nor to worship as we worship. No, we go to defend their right to worship as they please . . . and to tell them of a God worthy of worship.

Lieutenant Colonel Whitener said at lunch today, "These poor people out here are basically like us. All they want is peace, a decent home, an education for their children, and the right to worship freely." . . . Monday, Wednesday, and Friday our men teach English in native schools. They teach crowds. . . .

Whitener also said, "If anyone asks you why we do not withdraw our forces from Viet Nam, ask them if they would like the United States to be responsible for the deaths of three to six million South Vietnamese. "Charlie" would immediately massacre anyone who had any dealings whatever with our forces. See that waitress over there? (The girl was serving our lunch.) She would be shot because she worked in our compound." Yes, this business of killing in war *is* rather complicated. . . .

Our copter landed yesterday on what

looked like a football field with six inches of mud. Roy was wearing a beautiful, brand-new Stetson (white as the driven snow). The gale from the copter blades blew it off his head and half-way across the field. If he had seen or heard me laugh as he ran after it, I think he would have shot me on the spot.

Poor Roy. How the man suffers! The last night in Viet Nam—in Saigon—we were nearly jolted out of our beds by a terrific explosion followed by three minor explosions. They sounded about a block away. I invoked the Lord's protection immediately, as I jumped up, ran over, and shook Roy awake. "What was *that?*" I demanded. Hardly opening one eye, he murmured, "An explosion, I guess." I shook him again. "Wake up and *talk* to me!" He opened the other eye and said, "Hello." That was the night I could have shot *him*.

The explosions were at a fuel depot where we had put on a show our second day in Viet Nam.

It will be a relief to start home tomorrow. I will be a lot safer in California, but having

I receive a bouquet presented by Sp/4 Freeman on behalf of all the servicemen attending the performance at the Saigon USO (Dale Evans-Roy Rogers Show; USO-Hollywood Overseas Committee Tour).

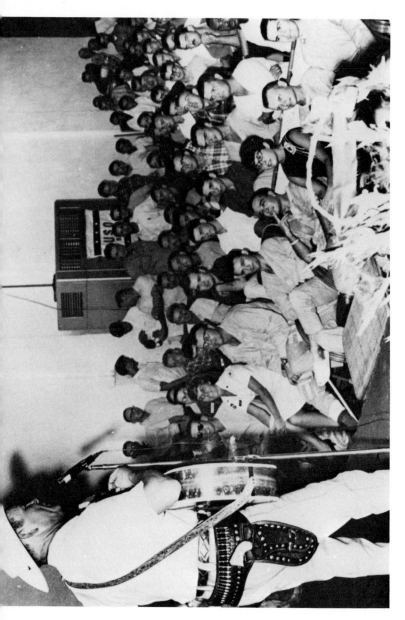

Roy entertains an audience which includes patients from the nearby Seventeenth Field Hospital in Saigon (Dale Evans-Roy Rogers Show; USO-Hollywood Overseas Committee Tour).

General Westmoreland and Captain Jagielski after the presentation of citations "For Service to Morale of Armed Forces in SE Asia" to Roy, Wayne West, the Travelons and me in General Westmoreland's office in October, 1966.

"... some day I'll learn to drive a *real* tank."
Sandy Rogers, Private, United States Army.

been here, I know I will never be the same again.

Didn't realize how tired I was. We are airborne, flying home by way of Japan and Alaska. The letdown is hard to describe.

* * * *

* * * Sandy

My prophecy that Sandy would "never be home again" didn't come 100 percent true; he did come once, during his early training days, on short leave—long enough to see his friends and his highly special friend, Sharyn. They became officially engaged, then back to camp for Sandy. He knew three camps, in those days: Polk in Louisiana, Leonard Wood in Missouri, and finally Fort Knox in Kentucky. The day he was graduated from basic training at Polk he was in seventh heaven, and I was up there, too, for this was real accomplishment for the boy who had to fight so hard for everything. The captain of his outfit said to me, "In all my eighteen years experience in service, I've never seen a boy so anxious to become a soldier—never one who tried so hard."

He asked for no favors because his Dad was Roy Rogers; he just wanted to be one of them, and make it on his own. At Leonard Wood he volunteered for demolition squad, which was about as dangerous a job as he could find. He was turned down. He could swim like a fish, but his reactions were much too slow for such a job. At Knox he volunteered for Viet Nam. Turned down. I wondered why, in view of his accomplishment at Fort Knox. It has been explained to me in a language that makes sense: "We couldn't let him risk his life in Viet Nam. You see, guerilla fighting out there is vicious, and fast. A man has to think quickly and act quickly, and Sandy was slow in that department. We knew he couldn't last very long in Viet Nam." So they shipped him out to Germany.

I flew to Fort Knox to say goodbye; in the middle of our talk he broke down and told me that on his eighteenth birthday he had gone on a "beer-bust" with some of his pals, to celebrate. So far as I know, he never drank even beer, before this, and it made him deathly sick. He was ashamed of it, bitterly ashamed. I could only remind him of his responsibilities for his actions as a Christian, and to the girl he planned to marry. I shook with fear, inside, that he might have inherited a weakness for alcohol, but I kept it to myself. He was determined to stay clear of liquor, and I did my best to strengthen that determination.

Just after this he wrote to us:

Mom and Dad: I'll make this promise to both of you—that when Sharyn and I get married and raise our kids, they will be raised in a home where Christ is Lord. That old saying, 'A family that prays together stays together,' goes for both of us. We will try our hardest to raise our kids as God wants them raised. It's tough that I didn't finish high school in civilian life, but I'm going to finish it in the Army, and I'll make you both, and everyone else, proud of me. . . . I realize that it isn't much of a jump from being seventeen to being eighteen, but I have finally realized that parents aren't just talking to hear their heads rattle, when they're trying to tell us something. All the time, kids think they're smart and their parents are dumb, but it's just the opposite: parents are the smart ones and the kids are the dumb ones. Some day, when I have my own kids, I hope I can show them the patience that you've shown with me and the other kids. God bless you both, always. Love, Sandy

He wrote Dr. Larry White, the minister at the Chapel in the Canyon:

Tell the gang at the Chapel I hope they all enjoy school very much (joke!)—but to be serious, tell them to be smart and *stay* in school, and not quit like me, and *don't give up*. God bless you all.

Sandy the Rebel

In his first letter from Germany, he said he had volunteered for Viet Nam again and still hoped to be sent there "to preserve the freedom of my country and the freedom of the people in Viet Nam." If I heard him say that once, I heard it a hundred times; these were words cut deep into his heart.

It was really tough for him in Germany, and he had more goofs than victories. He made a million mistakes, but he always came back for more, and he won the respect of his buddies and his officers, even when they were impatient with his blundering. He'd clown when he blundered, as he had clowned that night in the show when he had goofed on his line. His sergeant told me, in Viet Nam, "I was mad enough to kill him, a hundred times, when he put on that crazy comedy act. If I had only known what I know now!" Only known about the beatings he took as a baby, about the brain damage. . . .

In spite of it all he managed (I'll never know how) to get into the tank corps! I couldn't believe it, but there he was: the little boy who had played with his tanks on the living-room floor and who said, "Some day I'll drive a tank. A big one." He had a big one. He loaded and unloaded it, drove it, loved it. He wrote us:

Wednesday night the gunner of the tank I drive almost got crushed to death by the main gun when it accidentally lowered on him. But the full weight of the gun (2470 pounds) didn't get him, because, you see, he only comes to just about my shoulders, and so the gun rested on the periscope box, and he only got a busted jaw and a badly sprained neck; if he had been my size he would have been crushed to death. I'll tell you all now: I really knew the power of prayer, and I did some tall praying that night. I prayed he wouldn't die, because he looked real bad for awhile. But God is great and God is good and He takes care. Will you do me a favor and pray for him?

Things seemed to be breaking for him, at last. He had made it to the driver's seat in the tank, against almost impossible odds, and his letters bubbled with optimism for the future. He was even happier when he was promoted to Private First Class; his joy knew no

[104]

bounds. He wrote us: "Put your faith in the Lord because (as I have found out) He's always around when you need Him. All He asks in return is your heart and devotion." He was all out in his devotion, and that was all we could ask. Go, boy!

Late in October, I went down to visit my parents in Italy, Texas, to celebrate my birthday with them. On the night of the thirtieth, I had one of the worst dreams of my life. I saw a horse fall with his rider, and roll over and over down a steep embankment. It was death with a capital "D," and I woke in a sweat of terror. I was still reliving that dream when I took a plane home. When I stepped out of the plane in Los Angeles, I looked across the Los Angeles International Airport and saw Marion and Cheryl at the gate. Why? They didn't do that very often, for I flew a lot and they had too much to do at home, but there they were, and they weren't laughing. There was a strange expression on their faces. I knew instantly that something had happened. I ran to them and asked, "What is it? Who is it?" Cheryl said, "It's

Sandy, Mom." She almost whispered, "He's dead, Mom."

Everything spun around me, like a million tops gone crazy. I shouted, "No. Not Sandy! No!" Roy and Dusty came up, and they got hold of me, and led me into a corner of the lounge. When I quieted down they told me the story. . . .

He had come back from twenty-six days of maneuvers with his company, dog tired. That night there was one of those celebrations. They had to "wet down the stripes" of PFC Rogers, in the old Army tradition. So he and his buddies showered, picked up their pay, and went to the enlisted men's club for dinner. One of them was one of those hard-boiled, cynical, boastful, and bullyish fellows you find everywhere, on such occasions; I understand he needled Sandy with the words, "So now you're PFC. Now you're a man. Or are you? Let's see you drink like a man. Let's see if you can hold it, Rogers." And Sandy fell for it. He wanted to prove himself as good as the rest of them—as good as this loud-mouthed braggart.

With a pal, he polished off a full bottle of champagne; then they had two cocktails; then steak dinner, followed by *four* Zombies (a concoction made up of whiskey, gin, vodka, and brandy), topped off with a sweet cordial. "Come on, Rogers. Bottoms up!" Sandy, who had never tasted anything stronger than beer, poured it down. To be accepted, he drank that! He collapsed. They made him vomit as much as possible, but it was not enough. They got him into his bunk, where he slept, and they thought he would be all right.

In the morning they found him dead in his bunk.

It was wrong—terribly, fatally wrong. None of us ever dreamed he could do a thing like this. At first, I was blind with grief and rage. *Why did the Army let it happen?* Why was it so easy for these boys to get this liquor? Then it dawned upon me the Army couldn't stop it. If a soldier wants booze, he can always get it, one place or another, in or near his post or camp. John Barleycorn is a most persistent camp follower.

This I know, too: such temptations come to all of us as we grow up, in greater or lesser degree. We can give our children the finest training in the world, give them all the love we have, do everything we can to make them grow strong, straight, and ten feet tall, but when you take a boy out of such an environment of love, and cut him off from all the normal contacts of childhood, youth, and a good home, and subject him to such temptations under the conditions of war, it can all be destroyed in a matter of minutes. It is hard enough for a strong-willed, normal boy to fight it off; it is a lot harder for a boy like Sandy.

I am not offering excuses, but I am trying to explain. What happened was all wrong. Sandy was wrong, in accepting the dare to "drink like a man." It should never have happened like this, but it did, and I explain what happened and why in the hope that some other boy, so tempted, may find the strength to resist and conquer it.

The waiting for Sandy to come home was hard. We put away the toys; we put away his letters, and we walked in almost melancholy silence through a silent, whispering house. It seemed that every time we turned around, we saw something that reminded us of Sandy. We called up all the strength and faith we had, to face the dark day of his coming. And at long last, it came.

We drove out to Forest Lawn Cemetery and walked into the Church of the Recessional. Here we had said "goody-bye" to Robin and to Debbie; here, now, was the flag-draped casket of our Sandy. There was a service mercifully short, and we followed him out through the doorway to the church yard. A military escort walked ahead of us; a bugler blew "Taps," and from the rifles of the escort there cracked out a sharp salute. It was then, and only then, that Roy broke; he stood there thinking of the days when he had tried to teach Sandy to shoot, on the target range, and of how hard the boy tried to master it. Now—so late, so tragically,—but now, he had mastered it.

The flag was taken from his casket, folded in the traditional ceremony, and handed to me, his mother. I held it to my heart, held him to my heart, and then we turned away, and left him with God.

The Lord gave, and the Lord hath taken away; blessed be the name of the Lord. (JOB 1:21)

Rest in peace, sweet Kentucky babe!

EPILOGUE

I would be less than honest if I were to pretend that Sandy's death did not shake me, and that the manner of his passing was not hard. But if you wonder whether I have come to the place where I think that all this long struggle of Sandy toward a goal he never reached—that it has all ended in bitter disillusionment and defeat, or if you think that my faith has been broken or destroyed by his mistaken acceptance of an unworthy challenge in Germany, let me repeat to you the words of St. Paul to the Romans: "For I am persuaded, that neither death, nor life, nor angels, nor principalities, nor powers, Nor things present, nor things to come, nor height, nor depth, nor any other creature, shall be able to separate us from the love of God, which is in Christ Jesus our Lord"

(ROMANS 8:38, 39). *Nothing* could separate me, or Sandy, from that.

This was tragedy, yes—tragedy hard to understand, and harder to accept. But tragedy, in a Christian's life, is a refiner, given that the dross and impurities may be cut away, leaving the pure gold of truth and true character. Blessed be the refiner's crucible! Blessed is the cross of Christ! Blessed is He who said, "If any man will come after me, let him deny himself, and take up his cross, and follow me. For whosoever will save his life shall lose it: and whosoever will lose his life for my sake shall find it." (MATTHEW 16:24, 25). And "The disciple is not above his master. . . . It is enough for the disciple that he be as his master . . ." (MATTHEW 10:24, 25). As I understand this, He meant that if we would be perfected unto our potential and grow in His likeness, we must *expect* trials, and with them the gift of His grace to bear them. If we never exercised our muscles, they would become flabby; even so, we must continually exercise the arm of faith so that it becomes strong enough to handle harder and harder tests. When we go to school as children, we do not expect the lessons to become easier as we go along; they become more difficult as we progress, *but we learn how to handle them.*

A dear old lady said to me once, "Remember that the Lord always fits the back to the burden." I buy that. He has done it for me. The more sorrow I have experienced, the more I have been able to appreciate the joys of life. If we had no hardships, how would we appreciate the blessings? If there is no ploughing and watering of the field, how can the tender shoots spring up out of a dry and thirsty ground? God has not promised us an easy way, but *peace* at the center of the *hard* way. Our Shepherd knows His sheep. They hear His voice, and are assured that He sees, understands, protects—and yet allows lessons for growth.

Of course, I do not fully understand Sandy's death, nor why one who wanted to give his life for his country could give it to a bottle. I do not understand why it should be possible for a boy of eighteen to come by so much hard liquor, in one night, and it is my prayer that action may be taken to prevent such a tragedy from striking down another boy in the future, in the same way. But this I do know: that I have seen every one of my children accept Christ and struggle to live His way, in the sublime faith that God cares for His own, and that not a sparrow falls from heaven but the Father knows and cares —cares enough to lift fallen, repentant man into eternal company with Him—cares enough to lift our struggling Sandy into the perfection he struggled for here. Blessed resurrection! I have no fears about the future life of Sandy, who fought a great fight. . . .

Nor do I fear for my own future, after all the tragedy that has struck our home. The clouds of sorrow have been thick and heavy, but they have always cleared away. I have reached the point of no return, in my Christian experience, and with Job I can cry, "Though he slay me, yet will I trust in him" (JOB 13:15).

A well-known TV personality, interviewing me when we published our *Dearest Debbie* book, said something like this: "You know, when you adopt children, as you and Roy have done, you just might be *asking* for troubles and heartache. Of course you can have that with your own children, but when you go out of your way to take in other children, you are, more or less, asking for it, aren't you?"

She had something there—some of the truth, but not all of it. A tree extends its branches and grows in grace, beauty, and strength when it strikes its roots down deeper, in standing against the winds and the storms that beat upon it. The same thing happens to us as human beings. We are strengthened when, doing our best for our natural children, we see them grow "in wisdom and stature, and in favour with God and Man" (LUKE 2:52). Roy and I have been strengthened even more in doing our best for those who, through no fault of their own, would never know the love of a home and a family, unless we brought it to them—even though sometimes it ends in tragedy that we cannot understand. *We live and we grow as*

[115]

we give. God asks us to go the *second* mile
. . . ! When we know how far Christ went for
us, a mere second mile doesn't seem too
much.

We miss Sandy, terribly. So do his friends;
their name was legion. At the Chapel in the
Canyon, near a beautiful tree, near a singing
fountain splashing in the sun, there is a
bronze plaque bearing words that describe
him well, and that give me a renewed
strength, peace, and understanding whenever
I read them:

John David (Sandy) Rogers
   Here he played. Here he prayed.
   Here he loved, and was loved by all.

You see, there was a strength in him that has
created strength in us.

As we flew home from Viet Nam, we gazed
down in farewell upon the land and the people he longed to help; and as we passed over
Japan I looked down from my window upon
Mount Fujiyama—majestic, snow-capped,
strikingly beautiful, somehow eternal. So, I

thought, stands the undaunted, undiscouraged spirit of the America he loved—triumphant over mountains of injustice, bigotry, greed, selfishness, apathy, and encroaching Godless materialism. I salute you, Sandy Rogers, PFC: you who saw it all so clearly—you who have made us see it more clearly, too.